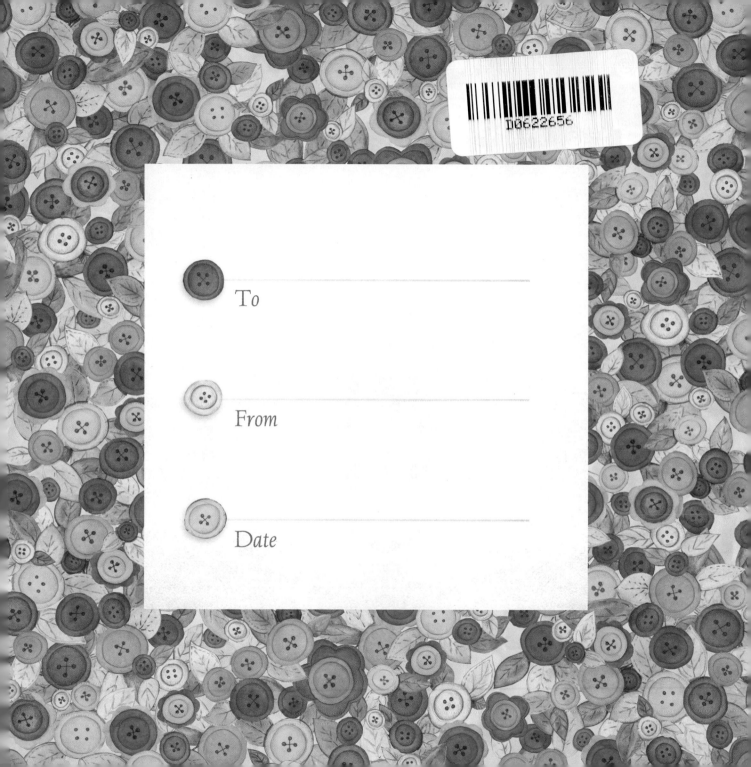

To _____

From _____

Date _____

SWEET COMFORTS OF HOME

Artwork by SUSAN WINGET

HARVEST HOUSE PUBLISHERS

EUGENE, OREGON

Sweet Comforts of Home

Text copyright © 2012 by Harvest House Publishers
Artwork copyright © 2012 by Susan Winget

Published by Harvest House Publishers
Eugene, Oregon 97402
www.harvesthousepublishers.com
ISBN 978-0-7369-2962-2

The artwork of Susan Winget is used by Harvest House Publishers, Inc. under authorization from Courtney Davis, Inc. For more information regarding art prints featured in this book, please contact:

Courtney Davis, Inc.
304 Main Street
Franklin, Tennessee 37064
www.courtneydavis.com / www.susanwinget.com

Design and production by Garborg Design Works, Savage, Minnesota

Printed in Singapore

12 13 14 15 16 17 18 / IM / 10 9 8 7 6 5 4 3 2 1

How good is man's life,
the mere living!
How fit to employ all the
heart and the soul and
the senses forever in joy!
Robert Browning

THE SWEET COMFORTS OF HOME

A Home Seasoned with Love

The word "home" inspires sweet memories and smiles of gratitude. For many, home is the

- happy refuge where the **sight** of a loved one warms the soul
- peaceful shelter, filled with the **scent** of vanilla candles, that beckons you to cozy up
- welcoming space where bear hugs and encouraging words make you **feel** forever cherished
- stress-free sanctuary humming with the **sound** of laughter and teakettle whistles
- gathering place overflowing with favorite **tastes** like apple pie and sugar cookies

Fill your every sense with the pleasures of home. Nestle into the haven of artist Susan Winget's beautiful paintings and linger over "a few of her favorite things." Savor those thoughts about what makes a house a home and a moment a memory.

BEAUTIFUL SIGHTS

Home, the spot of earth supremely blest, A dearer, sweeter spot than all the rest.

ROBERT MONTGOMERY

When you allow your heart to swell with sweet thoughts of home, what pictures come to mind? Do you see family gatherings around the kitchen table, the lush garden view from the patio, or the celebration of your child's first steps?

These are special times and experiences to recall often and remember always. They are blessings to inspire us when we are discouraged, calm us when we are anxious, or simply cheer us when we're caught up in daily routine.

Bless a heart today—even if it's your own! Create a beautiful setting and invite the people you love to enjoy it. Then look forward to talking about it, drawing comfort from it, and smiling about this sweet memory for all the days to come.

Often I think of the beautiful town

That is seated by the sea;

Often in thought go up and down

The pleasant streets of that dear old town,

And my youth comes back to me.

HENRY WADSWORTH LONGFELLOW

A house is built of logs and stones,

Of tiles and posts and piers,

A home is built of living deeds

That stand a thousand years.

VICTOR HUGO

Those who give
Love...
Gather Love

*Never lose an
opportunity of seeing
anything beautiful,
for beauty is God's
handwriting.*

RALPH WALDO EMERSON

A few of her favorite things...

Watching the sun rise is so heartwarming. Every morning I awaken early to tend to the horses on our farm. After feeding them, they wander out to the pasture to graze. I love watching these majestic creatures as the sun emerges behind them.

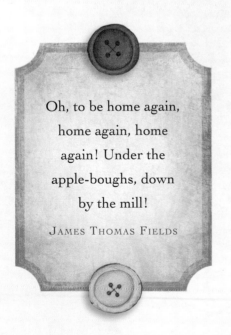

Oh, to be home again, home again, home again! Under the apple-boughs, down by the mill!

JAMES THOMAS FIELDS

So the short journey came blithely to an end, and in the twilight she saw a group of loving faces at the door of a humble little house, which was more beautiful than any palace in her eyes, for it was home.

LOUISA MAY ALCOTT, *An Old-Fashioned Girl*

Blest be that spot, where cheerful guests retire

To pause from toil, and trim their ev'ning fire;

Blest that abode, where want and pain repair,

And every stranger finds a ready chair.

OLIVER GOLDSMITH

Where we love is home,

home that our feet may

leave, but not our hearts.

OLIVER WENDELL HOLMES

CREATING HOMEMADE MEMORIES

- Set a garden bench in a just-right place to take in a beautiful view.
- Light a candle and place it in the window when expecting a loved one's arrival.
- Pick a handful of garden flowers to place in a vase by your daughter's or guest's bedside.
- Gather friends and family often to play games, eat cake, or watch a movie.
- Take lots of pictures, print the good ones, and display the best.

The ornaments of your house will be the guests who frequent it.

AUTHOR UNKNOWN

9

What colors come to mind when you think of your childhood home? The rich green of the neighborhood lawns, that favorite comfy sofa, or a first set of Tupperware canisters? The brilliant blue of marbles you collected, the dress Mom wore for her anniversary date with Dad, or the robin's egg you spotted in your favorite climbing tree? That charming color of pink of the old Westinghouse refrigerator, your first curlers, or the family's collection of Depression glass? What are the hues of your home today?

In our fifteen years of marriage, we've moved half a dozen times—always into fixer-uppers. Working while raising little ones in the midst of construction often made me feel grumpy—not at all like Mary, the perfect wife in *It's a Wonderful Life.*

During a particularly trying time, my husband told me, "No matter the situation, home is where we are together." At the time it sounded so cliché, but five kids later I know he's right. For now I am content in the midst of this chaos and noise because the sight of each other is home enough.

JEAN C.

A house without love may be a castle, or a palace, but it is not a home; love is the life of a true home.

JOHN LUBBOCK

O, *thou art fairer than the evening air clad in the beauty of a thousand stars.*

CHRISTOPHER MARLOWE

Home is a place not only of strong affections, but of entire unreserve; it is life's undress rehearsal, its backroom, its dressing room.

HARRIET BEECHER STOWE

SWEET SCENTS

The fragrance always stays in the hand that gives the rose.

GEORGE WILLIAM CURTIS

Breathe in deeply. Where does your heart take you? Does the soft scent of powder remind you of Grandma's gentle hug? Does the delicious aroma of fresh-baked bread, the Thanksgiving turkey, or birthday cake forever seat you at the family table and fill your spirit with happiness?

It's been proven that scents not only trigger memories, they evoke *emotional* memories. That's why having pleasant fragrances in our homes can fill us with feelings of peace, contentment, and joy. Think about those occasions when you searched for and prepared that special spicy recipe, handpicked a bountiful, sweet-smelling bouquet, or spritzed on a favorite perfume. Do you smile when you smell fresh coffee in the early morning or cuddle up in clean linens at night? These are such simple ways to infuse a home and a life with goodness and joy.

Lovely flowers
are the smiles of
God's goodness.

WILLIAM WILBERFORCE

Far from the city's dust and heat,
I get but sounds and odors sweet.
Who can wonder I love to stay,
Week after week, here hidden away,
In this sly nook that I love the best —
This little brown house like a ground-bird's nest?

ELLA WHEELER WILCOX

Behave so the aroma of your
actions may enhance the general
sweetness of the atmosphere.

HENRY DAVID THOREAU

Nothing can cure the soul but
the senses, just as nothing can
cure the senses but the soul.

OSCAR WILDE

Delicious (and drinkable) Potpourri

Enough apple cider to fill a large kettle

One apple, cut horizontally to make circular round slices, 1/2-inch thick

One orange, cut into round slices, 1/2-inch thick

3 whole cinnamon sticks

6 whole cloves

6 whole allspice berries

One 2-inch piece of fresh gingerroot, cut into small rounds

Place all ingredients in a large kettle and bring to a simmer. Reduce heat and allow to simmer uncovered, adding apple cider as liquid evaporates. To serve, ladle into mugs.

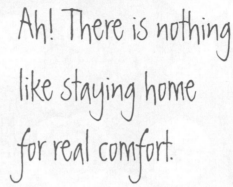

Home is the resort
Of love, of joy, of peace
and plenty, where,
Supporting and supported,
Polish'd friends,
And dear relations mingle
into bliss.

JAMES THOMSON

Ah! There is nothing
like staying home
for real comfort.

JANE AUSTEN, *Emma*

CREATING HOMEMADE MEMORIES

- Plant fragrant flowers close to the front door; consider roses, hyacinth, lilacs, or lavender.

- Choose a favorite perfume, make it your "signature" scent, and wear it often.

- Place scented candles around your home and light them frequently.

- Mix three to four drops of a favorite essential oil in a spray bottle filled with water, shake to mix, and spray to refresh stale air.

- Keep frozen cookie dough on hand to bake just before guests arrive. Fresh-baked cookies fill the house with a delicious aroma and are a welcomed treat for your friends.

It is a golden maxim to cultivate the garden for the nose, and the eyes will take care of themselves.

ROBERT LOUIS
STEVENSON

I go to nature to be soothed and healed, and to have my senses put in order.

JOHN BURROUGHS

17

> O bserve, record, tabulate, communicate. Use your five senses. Learn to see, learn to hear, learn to feel, learn to smell, and know that by practice alone you can become expert.
>
> WILLIAM OSLER

Show me another pleasure like dinner which comes every day and lasts an hour.

CHARLES MAURICE DE TALLEYRAND

When the kindling first catches on fire and the flames start licking at the logs, that's when the wonderful smoky scent drifts into the air. I inhale deeply and am instantly reminded of my father and the contentment I enjoyed as a child when I curled up next to him on cold winter evenings. He was the one to set the logs, light the fire, and carry the aroma back to me. It was on his hands…and I loved how they encircled me with love.

PEGGY W.

A HOUSE IS MADE OF WALLS AND BEAMS;

A HOME IS BUILT WITH LOVE AND DREAMS.

Author Unknown

20

TENDER TOUCHES

I want to touch the heart of the world and make it smile.

CHARLES DE LINT

A touch can bring refreshment. Think of a cool, damp cloth on your fevered forehead. A touch can rally deep emotion. Imagine a mother's first embrace of her newborn. A touch can also be so ordinary that it almost goes unnoticed. Do you remember how the fresh morning air felt on your face when you stepped outside this morning?

We touch things to learn about our world, relate to each other, and experience pain and pleasure. When you lift a delicate teacup to take that first sip of tea, you instantly understand much—you learn that the teacup is fragile and light, round in shape, smooth to the touch, and very warm because it holds hot tea. You also *feel* blessed by the experience—a dear friend has invited you to her table to share a cup of tea and cozy conversation. What could be better?

Isn't it time you fill your home with tactile joys? Bring out the Play Doh and urge those little ones to squish it up. Cuddle up on the couch with a comfy blanket and lots of fluffy pillows. Be a hugger and practice often! Positive touches, though they may last only a moment, can linger in the memory forever.

At the touch of love everyone becomes a poet.

PLATO

Our natural and happiest life is when we lose ourselves in the exquisite absorption of home…

DINAH MARIA MULOCK

A few of her favorite things...

I have always loved the art of quilting. I am blessed to have a few of my grandmother's quilts—precious heirlooms that are full of history and made with love. Last year my daughter Erin made her very first quilt and gave it to me on Mother's Day. It is one of the most thoughtful gifts I have ever received, and wrapping up in this beautiful quilt makes me think of her and all the sweet memories we've shared.

Sit with me at the homestead hearth,
And stretch the hands of memory forth
To warm them at the wood-fire's blaze.

JOHN GREENLEAF WHITTIER

Sweet is the hour that brings us home,
Where all will spring to meet us;
Where hands are striving as we come,
To be the first to greet us.

ELIZA COOK

BLESSED IS THE INFLUENCE OF ONE TRUE,
LOVING HUMAN SOUL ON ANOTHER.

GEORGE ELIOT

> *Sunshine is delicious, rain is refreshing, wind braces up, snow is exhilarating; there is no such thing as bad weather, only different kinds of good weather.*
>
> JOHN RUSKIN

H appiness is as a butterfly, which, when pursued, is always beyond our grasp, but which, if you will sit down quietly, may alight upon you.

NATHANIEL HAWTHORNE

CREATING HOMEMADE MEMORIES

- Arrange a bookshelf in a common area and fill it with vintage hardcover poetry books.
- Collect stones from favorite destinations and display them in a glass vase. Reach in often to pick one out, hold it, and relive the special time spent in that wonderful place.
- Plant a flower bed or a vegetable garden. Digging in the dirt is almost as satisfying as harvesting the beautiful bouquet or basketful of vegetables.
- Gather and give away hugs, kisses, and smiles everywhere you go.
- Invite children into the kitchen to bake sugar cookies or make anything that gets their little hands in the dough and puts a little giggle in their hearts.

Clay Dough

1 cup flour
1 cup water
1/2 cup salt
2 tablespoons cream of tartar
1 tablespoon oil
Food coloring

*Optional: Lemon or orange
oil may be added to make the
dough more fragrant

Mix together. Cook on low
temperature, stirring constantly,
until it is "slick" and moves
away from edge of pan. Cool.
Keep sealed in plastic bag.

Children are the hands by
which we take hold of heaven.

HENRY WARD BEECHER

His heart was like a sensitive plant,
that opens for a moment in the
sunshine, but curls up and shrinks
into itself at the slightest touch of the
finger, or the lightest breath of wind.

ANNE BRONTE

*The happiest moments
of my life have been the
few which I have passed
at home in the bosom
of my family.*

THOMAS JEFFERSON

All God's pleasures are
simple ones; the rapture of a
May morning sunshine, the
stream blue and green, kind
words, benevolent acts, the
glow of good humor.

R.W. ROBERTSON

My childhood home didn't echo
with the warning *Don't touch that!*
My sister and I could wrap up in
the family quilts during Midwest
winters. We could close our eyes
and trace fingers around the raised
edging on our dinner plates and
guess whether they were the rose
or leaf patterns. And we could
reach for the hands of our mother
and father even if mud pie residue
was all over our own. Home should
always be an open invitation to
touch, to embrace life's simple joys.

HOPE L.

DISTINCT SOUNDS

We love music for the buried hopes, the garnered memories, the tender feelings it can summon at a touch.

LETITIA ELIZABETH LANDON

What sounds fill you with joy, make you smile, and give you a lift? Do you stop what you're doing to catch the sound of birds chirping just beyond the open window? Is a toddler's riotous belly laugh so captivating that you simply must join in? When the house is clean and the dinner is made, does the sound of the car pulling in to the driveway put a smile on your face?

Through a complicated process, our ears sense delicate changes in air pressure, which our brains then interpret and understand…a loved one's voice, the sweet music of a favorite lullaby, or the familiar creak of the back door opening. As days go by, sounds naturally become paired with emotions. That's why we feel safe and protected when the rain falls steadily on the roof above, enchanted when a child sings a sweet nursery rhyme, and happy when the sound of spirited conversation fills the house during the holidays.

Orchestrate a lovely sound in your home. Let the teakettle sing! Turn up the music. Create a reason to laugh out loud. And listen… Do you hear a sweet memory in the making?

When I hear music, I fear no danger. I am invulnerable. I see no foe. I am related to the earliest times, and to the latest.

HENRY DAVID THOREAU

30

A few of her favorite things...

My favorite hymn is "For the Beauty of the Earth" by Folliott S. Pierpoint. I sang it often as a child and came to love it even more when I discovered how special it was to my beloved father-in-law. Recently my daughter chose to have it sung at her wedding ceremony, making it even more precious. Every line of this hymn speaks to my heart and reminds me of life's blessings and the pleasures of being part of a loving family.

Dark is the night, and fitful and drearily
Rushes the wind, like the waves of the sea!
Little care I, as here I sit cheerily,
Wife at my side and my baby on my knee:
King, king, crown me king:
Home is the kingdom and love is the king!

WILLIAM RANKIN DURYEA

M usic is the fourth great material want, first food, then clothes, then shelter, then music.

CHRISTIAN NEVELL BOVEE

Home is the one place in all this world where hearts are sure of each other. It is the place of confidence. It is the place where we tear off that mask of guarded and suspicious coldness which the world forces us to wear in self-defense, and where we pour out the unreserved communications of full and confiding hearts. It is the spot where expressions of tenderness gush out without any sensation of awkwardness and without any dread of ridicule.

FREDERICK W. ROBERTSON

The tree of silence bears the fruit of peace.

ARABIAN PROVERB

CREATING HOMEMADE MEMORIES

- Play music as a sound track to your day…as you wake up, during your devotions, and while you cook, clean, and celebrate life unfolding.
- Hold a large seashell to your ear to catch the sound of the ocean whenever you wish.
- Record loved ones' voices often and make a collection to have and give to other family members.
- Quiet your mind, be still, and listen to the sounds of your home… laughter and sighs are the echoes of its very heart.

The sound of a kiss is
not so loud as that of a
cannon, but its echo lasts
a great deal longer.

OLIVER WENDELL HOLMES

May your
home always
be too small
to hold all of
your friends.

AUTHOR UNKNOWN

When the green woods laugh with the voice of joy,

And the dimpling stream runs laughing by;

When the air does laugh with our merry wit,

And the green hill laughs with the noise of it.

LORD BYRON

Popcorn Birthday Cake

12 cups popped corn (unsalted)
1 12-ounce package peanuts, no paper skins
6 tablespoons butter
1 10.5-ounce bag marshmallows
1 teaspoon vanilla
1/2 teaspoon salt
1 12-ounce package mini candy-coated chocolate pieces

Generously butter a tube (Bundt) pan and set aside.
Place the popcorn and peanuts in a very large mixing bowl.

In a saucepan over low heat, melt the butter and marshmallows together, stirring constantly so the mixture doesn't burn. Add the vanilla and salt and stir to blend. Immediately pour the mixture over the popcorn. Butter your hands and mix with your hands quickly. Add the mini chocolate pieces and finish mixing, still using your hands. Press firmly into the prepared cake pan and let stand for at least 1 hour.

When ready to serve, unmold the cake onto a serving plate and add candles.

*Let one who wants to move and convince others,
first be convinced and moved themselves. If a
person speaks with genuine earnestness the
thoughts, the emotion and the actual condition of
their own heart, others will listen because we all
are knit together by the tie of sympathy.*

THOMAS CARLYLE

Whenever my parents played their oldies, a hairbrush instantly became my microphone, and our living room my stage. I danced around the floor and moved my lips in time to the words, much to my mom's delight. In my youth I performed many a concert for her. Thirty years later when I hear those same songs, it takes me back to when I was her little superstar. I have always been amazed by the power of music and its ability to transport us to another time and place.

MARION J.

That man is a
success who
has lived well,
laughed often
and loved
much.

ROBERT LOUIS
STEVENSON

Of all the music
that reached
farthest into
heaven, it is
the beating of a
loving heart.

HENRY WARD BEECHER

ENTICING TASTES

> *There is an invisible garment woven around us from our earliest years; it is made of the way we eat, the way we walk, the way we greet people.*
>
> JEAN GIRAUDOUX

Grandma's oatmeal cookies, Mom's meatloaf and mashed potatoes, Auntie's cinnamon rolls. Just thinking about those yummy treats makes our mouths water, our minds stir up sweet memories, and our hearts yearn for home.

Although everyone can recognize the four basic tastes: sweet, salty, sour, and bitter, each person tastes those flavors a little bit differently. With a dip of the finger, a sip from the spoon, or a lick of the spatula, the good cook determines just the right flavors to please her guests. Cooking for those she loves becomes a tangible expression of her devotion to them.

Savor the flavors of home. Bake a recipe that's been handed down through the generations and enjoy the taste as well as the loving memories. Try a new exotic sauce to ladle over rice. Relish the distinct flavors. Relax at the table. Enjoy the food, the people, the experience. Take this sweet moment to heart and cherish the tastes of home.

*No matter what looms ahead, if you can eat today, enjoy
the sunlight today, mix good cheer with friends today, enjoy
it and bless God for it. Do not look back on happiness —or
dream of it in the future. You are only sure of today; do not
let yourself be cheated out of it.*

HENRY WARD BEECHER

Cheerfully share your
home with those who need
a meal or a place to stay.

THE BOOK OF FIRST PETER

It was the policy of the good old gentleman to make his children
feel that home was the happiest place in the world; and I value this
delicious home-feeling as one of the choicest gifts a parent can bestow.

WASHINGTON IRVING

A few of her favorite things...

Our family has been baking angel biscuits on the farm for generations. My mother-in-law and her sister, Aunt Martha, named them as such because they bake up so light and fluffy. The children could never get enough of their grandmother's beloved biscuits.

ANGEL BISCUITS

5 c. unsifted flour
1/4 c. sugar
3 tsp. baking powder
1 tsp. soda
1 tsp. salt

1 c. shortening
1 pkg. dry yeast
2 Tbsp. warm water
2 c. buttermilk

Sift dry ingredients together, cut in shortening. Dissolve yeast in warm water and add with buttermilk to dry ingredients. Mix well.

Turn out on lightly floured board, add more flour if necessary. Roll to 1/4 inch thickness. Brush with melted butter. Place on lightly greased baking sheet. Bake at 400 degrees for 15 minutes. This dough can be kept in refrigerator and used as needed or biscuits can be cut and put on aluminum foil, covered, and frozen until just before baking time.

SIT DOWN AND FEED, AND WELCOME TO OUR TABLE.

WILLIAM SHAKESPEARE

Acorns were
good until
bread was
found.

FRANCIS BACON

*A man seldom
thinks with more
earnestness of
anything than he
does of his dinner.*

SAMUEL JACKSON

Live in each season as it passes; breathe the air, drink the drink, taste the fruit, and resign yourself to the influences of each.

HENRY DAVID THOREAU

The Lord my pasture shall prepare,
And feed me with a shepherd's care;
His presence shall my wants supply,
And guard me with a watchful eye.

JOSEPH ADDISON

CREATING HOMEMADE MEMORIES

- Cardamom? Ras el hanout? Star anise? Bake a dish using spices you've never used before. Serve and savor the new tastes and inspired conversation.

- Start a new tradition. Discover a delicious new Christmas cookie recipe and bake a batch every year for family and friends.

- Call Grandma or Auntie and ask for that favorite recipe. Take time to reminisce about the reunions, family dinners, and celebrations of days gone by.

- Invite the family to choose a country and explore its culture through culinary tastes.

- Turn the tables and create a cozy winter picnic by serving soup and warm bread by firelight in the living room…or roasting marshmallows for s'mores around a snowy campfire in the backyard.

A mother's happiness is like a beacon, lighting up the future but reflected also on the past in the guise of fond memories.

HONORE DE BALZAC

Apple Coffee Cake

1 can apple pie filling (either a quart of your
  home-canned or a store-bought 20-ounce can)
2 eggs
1 cup oil
2 cups flour
1 teaspoon baking soda
1 teaspoon vanilla
2 cups sugar
1 teaspoon cinnamon
1 teaspoon salt
1 cup nuts, chopped

Combine all ingredients in a large mixing bowl
and mix well by hand. Pour batter into a greased
9 x 13-inch pan. (Optional: Before baking you
can sprinkle top with some granulated or brown
sugar.) Bake at 350° for 1 hour.

> Man could direct his ways by
> plain reason, and support his
> life by tasteless food, but God
> has given us wit, and flavor, and
> brightness, and laughter to enliven
> the days of man's pilgrimage.
>
> SYDNEY SMITH

I love the first sweet taste of summer strawberries. As a child, I looked forward to "pickin' days" with my mother and sisters. We'd go to the fields and slowly move down the rows, carefully choosing only the ripest berries to pluck and add to our pails. The hot sun on our backs and uninterrupted time with Mama always made the day seem special. To this day, I have only to taste a fresh-picked, sun-warmed strawberry, and I slip back to those carefree summer days when time was slow and Mama's joy filled our hearts like the berries in our buckets.

GEORGIA V.

Laughter is brightest where food is best.

IRISH PROVERB

Variety's the very spice of
life, that gives it all its flavor.

WILLIAM COWPER

Cheerful looks make every dish a feast,
and that it is which crowns a welcome.

PHILIP MASSINGER

Where thou art,
that is home.

EMILY DICKINSON

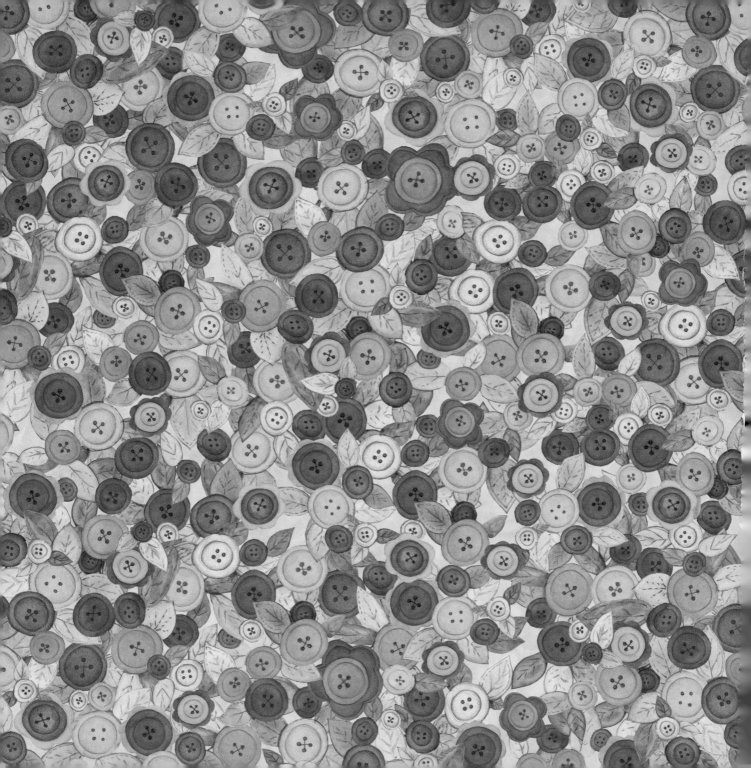